THE CROSS AT GROUND ZERO

THE CROSS AT GROUND ZERO

Fr. Benedict J. GROESCHEL, C.F.R.

Our Sunday Visitor Publishing Division
Our Sunday Visitor, Inc.
Huntington, Indiana 46750

*This little book is prayerfully dedicated
to all the victims of the terrorism
of the autumn of 2001
and their loved ones.*

Contents

A Word of Thanks

This book had to be prepared with great speed and in the midst of many other duties. In order for it to appear in a timely way, the cooperation of several people was essential.

First of all the very professional help of my skilled and patient editor, Charles Pendergast, was indispensable. He was assisted by our office staff, June Pulitano and Karen Killilea, and a dedicated priest friend who prefers to remain unnamed.

The series on which this book is based was part of the apostolate of the Eternal Word Television Network, a family I have been a grateful member of for twenty years.

I am also deeply grateful to Michael Dubruiel and other staff members at Our Sunday Visitor (including Henry O'Brien, the project editor) who literally came through with flying colors. Sherri Hoffman did a fine and thought-provoking design. Lisa Nash, who transcribed the original broadcast, was essential to the work, and lightning fast.

Mark Nelson of Nelson Woodcraft accepted my invitation to provide thousands of copies of the moving image of the Suffering Savior, which we then used as the visual theme of these meditations. To me, this painting by an unknown artist of the nineteenth century tells more about our Lord's care for us in sorrow than any words can do. I hope that you will get to know Nelson Woodcraft, whose address is given in this book on the copyright page.

Finally, I am grateful for the wonderful and almost mystical example of thousands of relatives of the victims: husbands and wives, parents and children, brothers and sisters who have shown such real faith and courage in these terrible times. The innumerable images of suffering faces that have filled the media tell us that there is still faith and love in America despite our own public image. If faith and love return to be the theme of

American life rather than selfish pleasure and greed, then indeed these suffering loved ones will have been God's instruments to bring good out of evil.

FATHER BENEDICT J. GROESCHEL, C.F.R.
THANKSGIVING 2001

Introduction

A huge twenty-foot cross, perfectly proportioned, was found in the mountain of debris at the ruins of the World Trade Center. The crossbeams had apparently been shaped by the collapse of the buildings. This cross has become a startling witness to faith for hundreds of thousands of people who were deeply grieved by the terrorist attacks not only in New York City but also in Washington and on the plane that crashed in Pennsylvania. This book, despite its title, is not about that metal cross. It is about the invisible but very real cross that fell on every innocent person, everyone whose heart was broken at Ground Zero on September 11, 2001.

Shortly after that date I was requested by Eternal Word Television Network, the international

Catholic cable network founded by Mother Angelica, to do four half-hour meditations on the events of that tragic day. These broadcasts were completed in less than three hours at the Instructional Television Center of the New York archdiocese on the grounds of St. Joseph's Seminary in Yonkers. My only preparation was to pray fervently to the Holy Spirit and prepare a simple outline during the twenty-minute drive over from Trinity Retreat, where I work. It seemed obvious that I should reflect on what this horror meant to individuals, to Christians, to the country, and to the world. I was remotely prepared because in my book *Arise from Darkness* (Ignatius Press, 1995) I had given much thought to the question "What do you do when life doesn't make sense?"

I hope and pray that *The Cross at Ground Zero* will be a help to all those who suffered in any way from the terrorism, even if they personally knew no one who died that morning. I also intend this book for those equally innocent people, most of them postal and office workers, who have contracted anthrax, as well as their families and friends. I write these lines in the presence of Christ in the Holy Eucharist. I also think of all those who will suffer in the future as a result of terrorism, which may continue. We pray that that may not be, but on this first Sunday of November, 2001, it seems that most thinking people believe that we may be in for a long period of suffering and sorrow, of violence and terror. May God give us peace.

The Warning

These four talks focus on two different themes, which are then repeated in each talk. I tried to make some spiritual observations about the meaning of suffering and the problem of evil — subjects of which I have some knowledge and experience. I also make certain observations about the need for America and the other Western nations to change radically from the self-destructive road we have chosen to travel, which is characterized by paganism, hedonism, and the corruption of youth. We have been on this road for some years, perhaps for more than three decades. As I read over the transcriptions of my broadcasts, I wondered if I had said these things. Did I have the courage, the insight, even the faith to say them? I was very tempted to modify my ideas. Then I recalled that I had asked for the guidance of the Holy Spirit, and I should not reject that guidance if it was given. Second, I was aware that Pope John Paul II had made the very same points in his address on September 12 concerning the terrorist attack (see Appendix One). He expressed in more gentle terms what I said, but he would have been obliged by his office to do that. However, if you read his words in Appendix One of this book, you will see that the supreme Shepherd of the universal Church was calling America to reform and repentance while he lamented what had happened to us.

From my recent visits to foreign countries and from reading and reviewing comments from writers even of friendly nations, it becomes clear that our national image is besmirched by our forceful advocacy of contraception, abortion, and euthanasia, and by our production of pornography, which constantly undermines family life and human dignity. I am reminded of the title of a book about America before World War II, which was made into a film in the 1960s — *Ship of Fools*. Are we Americans on such a ship? If we reap the harvest we have sown — and there is no reason to suppose that we will not — we cannot claim that we were not warned by the Bible and especially by the teaching of Christ, our own faith, and the supreme Shepherd of our Church. I am very critical of some of our former national leaders and their administration of justice, as well as their lack of care for our national security. I never thought I would write in such a vein, but the time to do so seems to have arrived.

Jesus gave many warnings to the people of His time. Even on His way to Calvary He warned the good, innocent women who were weeping for Him: "Daughters of Jerusalem, do not weep for me, but weep for yourselves and for your children. For behold, the days are coming when they will say, 'Blessed are the barren, and the wombs that never bore, and the breasts that never gave suck!' Then they will begin to say to the mountains, 'Fall on us'; and to the hills, 'Cover us' " (Luke 23:28-30). The destruction of Jerusalem and all Israel was still forty years off, and perhaps this explains the mysterious remark He then adds, "They do these things while the wood is green. What will they do when it is dry?"

The Meaning of the Cross

Many people ask why God did this. Some fundamentalist preachers have even suggested that He did, in fact, wreak vengeance on the United States for its sins. I find this to be a horrible idea — one that especially does not fit with the image of God provided by His beloved Son in the Gospel. Yes, God mysteriously permitted this evil, but as St. Augustine reminds us, "God does not do evil, but does cause that evil should not become the worst." I will try to explore further the idea that while God permits evil, He will bring good out of it for those who trust in Him. This is the meaning of the cross.

Jesus' death at the hands of brutal men was the worst sin ever committed, and it was inspired, we are told, by Satan as he entered Judas's heart. But by trust, love, forgiveness, and a total surrender to God's will that did not remove the cup of suffering, Jesus saved the world.

The cross is the symbol of the worst thing ever done and the best thing that ever happened. It is Christ's victory over death and our promise of eternal salvation.

The Presence

For believing and prayerful Christians, the cross is something more. It reminds us that Christ is present to us as we suffer. He is here. The French poet Paul Claudel reminds us that Christ did not end suffering or explain it away. He sanctified it by His presence. In these pages I will try to develop this idea because it represents the most powerful and uniquely Christian aspect of spirituality. The steel cross found in the ruins of the World Trade Center is a silent symbol of the presence of Christ with us. Because He suffered for us willingly in His life, He has a right to share our sufferings now. Only the believer can appreciate this. It will leave others puzzled and confused about what the cross means. But for the believer the cross stands still and the world turns all around it. It is the pole around which all things revolve. The quotation from Cardinal Newman in Appendix

Four at the back of this book will help the meditative Christian come to an appreciation of what the cross really means.

*O*ne

THE INDIVIDUAL

For to this you have been called, because Christ also suffered for you, leaving you an example, that you should follow in his steps. He committed no sin; no guile was found on his lips. When he was reviled, he did not revile in return; when he suffered, he did not threaten; but he trusted to him who judges justly. He himself bore our sins in his body on the tree, that we might die to sin and live to righteousness.

— 1 Peter 2:21-24

*M*any priests in the New York metropolitan area took turns to be of service at the morgue at the World Trade Center, and I went down one evening a couple of weeks after the terrorist attacks. We were about a block away from Ground Zero. All around us were huge piles of rubble, and a tremendous amount of work was going on with diggers and power shovels and bright lights, even in the middle of the night. My shift was from 6:00 P.M. to midnight, after which Brother Angelus, a deacon in our community, and I left, and two priests from Brooklyn came and took our place. At the morgue were a number of volunteer chaplains from around the country. There were Methodist ministers and Baptist ministers who had traveled to the site at their own expense, as well as Catholic priests and deacons, to see if they could be of help.

Our task was to conduct a short service each time the remains of a victim's body were brought into the morgue. In the course of those six hours we held a service eight times. Each time we prayed the twenty-third Psalm — "The Lord Is My Shepherd" — and recited The Lord's Prayer in the long form. We also read some of the Church's prayers for the dead, including the beautiful responsory *In Paradisum*:

> May the angels lead thee into paradise: may the martyrs receive thee at thy coming, and lead thee into the holy city of Jerusalem. May the choir of angels receive thee, and mayest thou have eternal rest with Lazarus, who once was poor.

After we had prayed, the medical examiner would try, with the help of a forensic anthropologist, to identify the various body parts and determine the person's age, sex, and any other characteristics for later identification. The remains were then frozen.

It was like standing at the Apocalypse.

All those reading this should know that almost every one of us in New York has had a personal stake in this tragedy. Each of us knows at least one family that has been deeply scarred by the events of September 11. Many friends, neighbors, and colleagues have lost very dear ones in the twinkling of an eye. America and much of the world grieved with us. Along with grieving, we have to learn something from this. In praying, reflecting, and discussing all that happened with many thoughtful people, I feel certain that we still have much to learn — as individuals, as a church, as a people, and as members of the human race.

Recently I spoke to Father Philip Eichner, S.M., president of Bishop Kellenberg Catholic High School in Uniondale, Long Island. The families of forty of the students at that school have been deeply affected by this tragedy. In some parishes, six, eight, ten, or more people have died. In a Middletown, New Jersey, parish twenty-three people are missing. I have been able to offer Mass and extend some consolation to a nearby family whose daughter was one of the September 11 victims. She had just been married for six months and was expecting a baby. In the midst of all this, it is impossible not to ask the question "Why?" And yet as real and perhaps necessary as it is to ask the question, it is difficult, if not impossible, to explain or answer satisfactorily.

There's nothing wrong with asking why. Jesus Himself asks why on the cross. The Son of God asks that very question. We read:

> From the sixth hour there was darkness over all the land until the ninth hour. And about the ninth hour Jesus cried with a loud voice, "Eli, Eli, lama sabachthani?" that is, "My God, my God, why hast thou forsaken me?"
>
> — MATTHEW 27:45-46

Why?

Let's stop and look at that question "Why?" Let's also ask the one that must come after it: "What?" What am I supposed to do in this tragedy? I saw that question being answered very clearly the night I was at Ground Zero and had the chance to observe the brave and generous men and women who were working there. Immense numbers of them were volunteers. They and those who were employed as police officers, fire fighters, and emergency personnel were working fifteen- or eighteen-hour shifts. Everyone was very respectful and cheerful, even though it was a dreadful scene. The Salvation Army provided all of us with a warm meal and candy bars. This entire group of people was doing a very fine job in those difficult circumstances.

We realize there is no adequate answer to the question "Why?" A devout rabbi who had lost his family at Auschwitz once advised me: "Don't answer questions for God." We are all trying to answer some easier questions: "What? What can I do? What am I supposed to do?"

I heard a story that unfolded at a funeral for one of the fathers who was killed in the terrible catastrophe. His little daughter, who was perhaps eleven or twelve years old, spoke at the end of the Mass. In so many words, she said, "I know what my father wants me to do. To learn. To do my studies. To graduate. To go to college. To be the best person my dad wants me to be." And there was great applause. This brave little girl was answering the question "What? What must I do?"

When we ask why, we should think of the suffering Christ. There is a hauntingly beautiful painting of Christ that many of my readers are familiar with and has been reproduced on the back cover as well as the beginning of each chapter of this book. It depicts Christ, crowned with thorns, being led out to death. At the bottom of the painting, a Latin inscription reads, "God so loved the world." The face is filled with sorrow. It is the face of the Son of God, suffering for our sins.

Let's look at the catastrophe and where it came from. Some people think it came from God. This could be consistent with some readings of the Old Testament, particularly the earlier books. We learn more about God in the Gospels. Our image of God grows clearer and becomes deeper until our Divine Savior says to Philip, "Have I been with you so long, and yet you do not know me, Philip? He who has seen me has seen the Father" (John 14:9).

We then come to this question: "Did God cause this catastrophe or any other evil?" St. Augustine answers the question by saying, "God does not do evil, but does cause that evil should not become the worst" (*Soliloquies*, 2). This is an interesting idea and one that is not often considered in the modern world. When this terrible attack occurred in New York, the two buildings were destroyed. It's quite possible, architects have told us, that the buildings might have fallen over sideways, as modern metal buildings sometimes do during an earthquake. They don't crumble — they just go over sideways. If that had happened, probably close to fifty thousand people would have died. It would have been terrible enough if just one innocent person had died. But evil did not become the worst. Those twin towers had forty thousand people working in them, and somehow most of them got out safely. There were many fire fighters, police officers, and emergency workers who did manage to survive. "God does not do evil, but does cause that evil should not become the worst."

But in a world which everyone can see is so beautiful, in a human race that is capable of such great acts of virtue, heroism, goodness, and beauty, we may well ask, "Why does evil occur at all?" Here we come up against the mystery of evil, or the mystery of darkness.

St. Thomas Aquinas says — and quite wisely,

I think — that most people who believe in God do so because of the problem of evil. And the reason most people who don't believe in God reject that belief is because of the same problem of evil. Belief or unbelief in Divine Providence depends on what you think about evil. Evil can take the form of an accident; for example, you fall down and break your leg. It can be a natural disaster, and you may be in the wrong place at the wrong time. When natural disasters occur, it is simply a question of nature — the natural world — operating according to its causes and effects.

In the case of a volcano, many people would say, "Wasn't it terrible that the volcano erupted?" If there were never any volcanoes, there wouldn't be any atmosphere on earth. So natural evils — even earthquakes, which can be devastating — are part of nature fulfilling its role. At the same time we hope we are not in the vicinity when earthquakes and other natural calamities occur.

People are often hurt in natural disasters because someone who might have been able to prepare them neglected to do so. We live in this gigantic material world, and you may get caught in the wrong place at the wrong time. Why does it happen? I don't know. I think when I get on the other side — that is, when I get to purgatory, because in heaven there will be no questions — I'd like to ask, "Why don't we have a lot of little volcanoes? Why don't we have little thunderstorms instead of hurricanes?" Since I've been at our retreat house on Long Island Sound, hurricanes have brought the sea into my office five times. Why? Because my office is built too close to the seawall.

Apart from the evil that occurs in nature, there are the evils that happen because of other people, and that's what we are dealing with here. Wicked, insane evil. Whatever prompted the evil aggression of September 11, whatever justification those who did it thought they had, whatever their motives, they attacked innocent, unsuspecting people. Many New Yorkers are completely puzzled by the choice of the World Trade Center as the target. The World Trade Center is not a symbol of anything to us. It's just another set of office buildings, and we don't take buildings very seriously. We have a lot of them. They're not symbols of anything. Working in those buildings that day were people who do represent financial interests, and they were no doubt working very hard to pay their mortgage. They were people who worked their way up the ladder, often starting in humble jobs. And there were other people who were doing the humble jobs. There were Christians, Jews, Muslims, Hindus, Buddhists, agnostics, and atheists. There were saints and sinners, and everyone in between. And then indiscriminately, with no warning and no personal responsibility for what was going on, they were iniquitously deprived of life. Some five thousand of them. At this writing, there is still a question as to the exact number of casualties.

The same thing happened at the Pentagon, and the same with those aboard the plane that crashed in Pennsylvania. And all the victims' families and children were plunged into sorrow. Wounds were inflicted that will leave horrible scars for a hundred years or more. Why did God permit such a thing to happen?

Nobody knows. Like all the other world religions, however, Christianity offers its own answer. The ancient religions reply, "Well, good and evil are part of life. They both come from God." Buddhism, which is considerably more sophisticated, makes the very good point, which is often true, that evil is in our eyes. We choose to identify the event that is going on as evil. Maybe, in fact, it isn't bad at all. It's like getting old. The worst news you could ever get is that you're not going to die for five hundred years. But there's no way to look at the recent attacks and say, "All the evil is just in my eyes." At least I cannot do that.

In Judaism the very important answer to why evil happens comes right from the Bible. It's in the book of Job.

Job was questioning God, as were his friends. And in the beginning of chapter 38 God shows up and answers Job:

> "Who is this that darkens counsel by words without knowledge? Gird up your loins like a man, I will question you, and you shall declare to me. Where were you when I laid the foundation of the earth? Tell me, if you have understanding. Who determined its measurements — surely you know! Or who stretched the line upon it? On

what were its bases sunk, or who laid its corner-stone, when the morning stars sang together, and all the sons of God shouted for joy? Or who shut in the sea with doors . . . ?"

— Job 38:2-8

And so God questions Job for several chapters. Finally Job says to the Lord:

"I know that thou canst do all things, and that no purpose of thine can be thwarted. Who is this that hides counsel without knowledge? Therefore I have uttered what I did not understand, things too wonderful for me, which I did not know."

— Job 42:2-3

And Job admits his error.

Job's answer has been examined from a modern point of view by Rabbi Harold Kushner in his book *When Bad Things Happen to Good People* (Schocken Books, 1981). But even in that book Rabbi Kushner mentions that for Christians there is another facet to the problem of evil. That aspect is the suffering Jesus Christ, whom Christians accept as the Son of God who was born into this world, Jesus Christ who endured the sufferings of human life and made Himself completely vulnerable.

I refuse to accept the interpretation that God willed the death of Jesus Christ, that God was responsible for the worst sin ever committed. On the contrary. Out of His infinite love God sent His Son to convert the world, to save the world, but human beings are free to accept Christ or reject Him. Oh, God knew very well — because He knows all things — that the Savior would not be accepted. But don't blame God for the death and crucifixion of Jesus Christ.

On September 11, I happened to be in Assisi, the city of St. Francis, giving a retreat to a group of priests, when the news came from the World Trade Center. We were all shocked. I couldn't pray. And when I cannot pray, I go to the nearest chapel and make the Stations of the Cross.

If you're not a Catholic, you may not be familiar with the Stations of the Cross; but perhaps you have seen on the walls of Catholic churches little statues or plaques commemorating the events of Jesus' Passion, death, and burial. There are usually fourteen, sometimes fifteen, of them. As I went to the first station on that terrible day, I was upset and angry. The question "Why?" was pounding in my brain. I admit I was angry. I don't like to say I was angry with God, because it's not very respectful. But if you do get angry with God, there are a couple of Psalms that are helpful.

> My God, my God, why hast thou forsaken me?
>   Why art thou so far from helping me, from
>   the words of my groaning?
> O my God, I cry by day, but thou dost not
>   answer;
>   and by night, but find no rest. . . .
> Yea, dogs are round about me;
>   a company of evildoers encircle me;
> they have pierced my hands and my feet —
> I can count all my bones —
>   they stare and gloat over me;
> they divide my garments among them,
>   and for my raiment they cast lots.
> But thou, O LORD, be not far off!

O thou my help, hasten to my aid!
Deliver my soul from the sword, my life from
the power of the dog!
Save me from the mouth of the lion,
my afflicted soul from the horns of the wild
oxen!

— Psalm 22:1-2, 16-21

O Lord, my God, I call for help by day;
I cry out in the night before thee.
Let my prayer come before thee,
incline thy ear to my cry!
For my soul is full of troubles,
and my life draws near to Sheol.

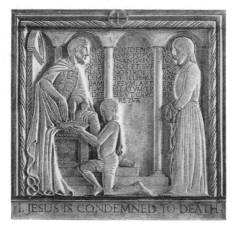

1. JESUS IS CONDEMNED TO DEATH

I am reckoned among those who go down to
　the Pit; . . .
But I, O LORD, cry to thee;
　in the morning my prayer comes before thee.
O LORD, why dost thou cast me off?
　Why dost thou hide thy face from me?
　　　　　　　　　　　— PSALM 88:1-4, 13-14

It may be that Jesus recited the whole of the
twenty-second Psalm on the cross. We know that
He said the first words of the Psalm.

At the first station I looked at the images and
thought of the scene of Jesus' condemnation:
Pontius Pilate washing his hands, the Scribes and
Pharisees, the Roman soldiers. They all wanted
the death of this utterly innocent man. And for
Christians, Christ is so much more than an utterly innocent man. He is the incarnate Son of
God. And who were condemning Him? Wicked
men. Stupid men. Men who were both wicked and
stupid at the same time. They were doing this to
Him. How many times in the history of the world
have wicked and stupid things been done? How
many times have people done wicked and stupid

things to the innocent? I think it's terribly important that we look into the face of the suffering Christ and see all the pain and agony there.

Of course, for so many people immediately affected by the tragedies, urgent questions had to be asked: "Was my daughter saved? Did my husband go to heaven? Will I see them again? Did they enter eternal life? Were they prepared?" These are important concerns, which take on even greater importance because you and I are going to die. We may die in some terrible accident. We may die in some hideous act of terror, or we may die in bed. But we will die, and we need to be prepared. Our Savior Himself warns us that He will return at a time we do not expect. We must be watchful and ready.

> "But of that day and hour no one knows, not even the angels of heaven, nor the Son, but the Father only. As were the days of Noah, so will be the coming of the Son of man. For as in those days before the flood they were eating and drinking, marrying and giving in marriage, until the day when Noah entered the ark, and they did

not know until the flood came and swept them all away, so will be the coming of the Son of man. Then two men will be in the field; one is taken and one is left. Two women will be grinding at the mill; one is taken and one is left. Watch therefore, for you do not know on what day your Lord is coming. But know this, that if the householder had known in what part of the night the thief was coming, he would have watched and would not have let his house be broken into. Therefore you also must be ready; for the Son of man is coming at an hour you do not expect.

— MATTHEW 24:36-44

St. Paul too has some sobering words for anyone who might be living complacently in a dream world and thinks that death and evil happen only to other people.

But as to the times and the seasons, brethren, you have no need to have anything written to you. For you yourselves know well that the day of the Lord will come like a thief in the night.

When people say, "There is peace and security," then sudden destruction will come upon them as travail comes upon a woman with child, and there will be no escape. But you are not in darkness, brethren, for that day to surprise you like a thief. For you are all sons of light and sons of the day; we are not of the night or of darkness. So then let us not sleep, as others do, but let us keep awake and be sober.

— 1 Thessalonians 5:1-6

The warnings from Scripture are clear: Learn from the recent tragic events visited on our country.

Because of cell phones, many people actually spoke to their dear ones on the upper floors of the World Trade Center before the buildings collapsed. Some who were on the airplanes spoke to their spouses at home. The very brave men who tried to take over the plane that crashed in Pennsylvania knew what was happening. Their families and loved ones at least have the memories of their last words: "I love you. God bless you."

I take great consolation from the fact that our

Divine Savior, who called us to a holy life, to walk on the straight way, and to enter by the narrow gate, also prayed at the very last moments of His life for those wicked and stupid men who were responsible for killing Him. He said, "Father, forgive them; for they know not what they do" (Luke 23:34). He prayed for the people who were killing Him. And we can be confident of their forgiveness, for in another place Jesus reminds us that the Father "hearest me always" (John 11:42). As Jesus was dying, there were two thieves crucified with Him. One of the thieves, a man from the street, a man under capital punishment who admitted he deserved his sentence, said, " 'Jesus, remember me when you come into your kingdom.' And [Jesus] said to him, 'Truly I say to you, today you will be with me in Paradise' " (Luke 23:42-43). It's quite possible for someone to call upon the name of the Lord in that last moment of life and be saved, for it says in Scripture, "It shall come to pass that all who call upon the name of the LORD shall be delivered" (Joel 2:32).

We Catholics have been very impressed in recent years by the revelations and mystical experiences of a humble Polish nun, St. Faustina Kowalska, a simple peasant woman who spoke and wrote a great deal about the divine mercy. She tells us that Jesus revealed to her that in His divine mercy He calls out to every soul in that millionth of a millionth of a second between life and death. He doesn't rely on us clergy. He doesn't rely on the Christians. He Himself calls every soul because He does not will the death of the sinner but wills that the person be saved. He has said: "As I live, says the Lord GOD, I have no pleasure in the death of the wicked [that is, the sinner], but that the wicked turn from his way and live; turn back, turn back from your evil ways" (Ezekiel 33:11). I take St. Faustina's revelations very seriously, and I have much hope. In Appendix Three of this book there is a passage from her diary in which she records a conversation revealed to her of Christ speaking to a despairing soul.

Look again at the image of the suffering Christ, the Man of Sorrows, on the back cover of the book. It will help you in dark times. And turn your focus from the question "Why?" Ask instead, "What do we do now?" Keep in mind too the

Scripture passages we have referred to. They should help you determine your course of action in the future. This is the answer to the question "What?" Prayer, vigilance, attention to spiritual duties, readiness in the life of the spirit, acts of charity and forgiveness — all these should be watchwords for every person of faith. We need not then fear a day of evil, an unexpected catastrophe, whether it be an occurrence of nature or the work of wicked men. And when our Divine Savior comes to call us home — however that summons is revealed — we can have great hope that we will hear these welcoming and calming words: "Come, O blessed of my Father, inherit the kingdom prepared for you from the foundation of the world" (Matthew 25:34).

Two

THE CHURCH

"Truly, truly, I say to you, he who hears my
word and believes him who sent me, has eternal
life; he does not come into judgment, but has
passed from death to life.
"Truly, truly, I say to you, the hour is coming, and
now is, when the dead will hear the voice of the Son of
God, and those who hear will live."
— John 5:24-25

*I*n this chapter I will focus on what the terrible events of September 11 mean to a member of the Catholic Church as well as to members of other Christian Churches. I will also consider what they mean to religious believers in general both in the United States and in the countries that are friendly to us. What is their significance to believers in a civilization like our own? I warn you that you may not be pleased with what I have to say, but I will be grateful if you will read it.

An observer of the passing scene in our society and culture for the last fifteen or twenty years once said to me, "There never was a bubble that didn't break." All sorts of people were expecting the bubble to break at that magical year, the millennium. Being an old New Yorker, I'm not into such things. The year 2000 was just another year in New York City. What does a number in the decimal system mean to God? But now a year later the bubble is breaking. Perhaps there are several bubbles, and only one of them has broken already. There are several things we can learn from this recent catastrophe. As I was working down at the morgue at Ground Zero, it became very clear that in the United States and in other Western countries we do not take seriously enough the fact that life is a journey, that not one of us is here to stay. We eat, drink, and are merry, and we forget what life is about.

In lower Manhattan, where terror struck, you could not miss the fact that human life is very fragile, that our security is almost an illusion, that nothing is absolutely safe. We all know we are going to die. Most of us are informed enough about medical facts to know that even in the body of a small child there may be catastrophic biological changes going on that will inevitably bring an early death. The events at the World Trade Center and at the Pentagon were catastrophic, but there are many other catastrophes every day that are not so dramatic.

It seems to me that religion in general in the United States has not reminded people of the fragility of human life, of the illusion of security in this world, of the folly of putting our trust and hope in material goods and human promises, as if we were not destined for something much better than this world. In short, religion has neglected to remind us that "we have here no abiding city." I don't want to be too critical of religion, because religion to some extent reflects the society in which it exists. But religion should do more than be a mirror. When my family used to complain about our pastor, I think I remember my Irish great-grandmother, Susie Murphy, saying, "The people get the clergy they deserve."

People get the clergy they produce, and people of various denominations, including my own, have expressed disappointment that some of the clergy were not up to this particular situation. Who was? Some complained that the churches and religions didn't prepare us for it. Who would have listened if they had tried to? Let me ask a question of churchgoers. Suppose your minister, priest, or rabbi got up and warned you, "Vanity of vanities, all is vanity except to those who love God and serve Him alone"; "Seek first the Kingdom of God and His justice and all these things will be added unto you"; "Blessed are the poor in spirit, for theirs is the kingdom of heaven. Blessed are those who mourn, for they shall be comforted. Blessed are those who suffer persecution for justice's sake, for theirs is the kingdom of heaven." Would we have listened? Or would it have been as the prophet said (see Isaiah 6:10), that God blocks our ears? That hearing, we may not hear. It is very important that each one of us think seriously about the questions this catastrophe raises.

Americans in leadership positions, especially religious leaders, should be aware that much of the world is scandalized by our moral behavior. We are a scandal as a nation. We export pornography by the ton — literature, electronic pornography, disks, movies, everything. The public media in our country are a septic tank of toxic waste. People have been very anxious about the possibility that terrorists will poison the reservoirs. Believe me, they are already poisoned, not by foreign terrorists but by our fellow Americans who bring into our living rooms poison and toxic waste that will destroy the moral lives of children and lead them into sexual relationships that are the furthest thing from a faithful marriage. TV and the Internet are used to corrupt values to such an extent that many of our young people have practically none at all. This has been going on for many years.

I am disappointed in organized religion in the United States and in us clergy because we have not made loud, powerful, public statements against pornography. It's toxic waste. By pornography I do not mean simply sleazy magazines. I mean the whole unhealthy use of the media to reduce human beings to mere objects of sexual gratification. Jesus says, "Do not fear those who kill the body but cannot kill the soul; rather fear him who can destroy both soul and body in hell" (Matthew 10:28). We have slayers of the soul all over the place, and moral death and destruction rain down on us, entering our homes through television and music. Some of the music stations that are designed for a teenage audience are absolutely vicious. I am told by people who occasionally monitor these stations that the advertisements, music, lyrics, and the whole message is one of fornication, exploitation, and total corruption of the young. Why is it that a class-action suit is not brought against many organizations in the media for the corruption of the morals of minors?

Immediately after the attack of September 11 Pope John Paul II made this important statement to James Nicholson, the new United States ambassador to the Holy See:

> Young people are surely your nation's greatest treasure. That is why they urgently need an all-round education which will enable them to reject cynicism and selfishness and to grow into their full stature as informed, wise, and morally responsible members of the community.
>
> At the beginning of a new millennium young people must be given every opportunity to take up their role as "craftsmen of a new humanity, where brothers and sisters — members all of the same family — are able at last to live in peace" (Message for the 2001 World Day of Peace, 22).
>
> — "AMERICA'S MORAL POTENTIAL,"
> THE HOLY FATHER'S ADDRESS
> OF SEPTEMBER 13, 2001

In addition to the fact that we all but ignore the pornography in our midst, we do not raise our voices against the killing of the innocent. From personal experience and contacts with the United Nations, I know that the nations that oppose abortion and euthanasia, joining their voices to that of the Holy See, are for the most part Muslim nations. The Muslims are scandalized by our abuse of family life, by our abuse of the unborn. Who is saying anything?

Recently, former President Clinton, who forcefully supported partial-birth abortion while in office, said in a broadcast related to this tragedy that he was particularly concerned about children who are unborn. *Children who are unborn!* Yes, I wish that we in this country would get concerned about children who are unborn and understand that they are children. In the United States and generally in the Western nations, we need to grow up and face the biological and medical fact that we legally kill children who are unborn.

It is about time that religion in this country prepared itself to be a little unpopular. If you read the New Testament, as well as the Jewish scriptures, which we Christians call the Old Testament, you will see that very often religious people have failed to raise their voices against evil and the violation of God's laws in their midst. There is a passage from St. Luke's Gospel that is appropriate to the recent attacks of terror in our country. It brings out the role of clergy and Christian leaders, as well as the fact that we can fail in our duty just as the apostles did. At the Last Supper, right before Jesus is arrested, He addresses the apostles:

> "You are those who have continued with me in my trials; as my Father appointed a kingdom for me, so do I appoint for you that you may eat and drink at my table in my kingdom, and sit on thrones judging the twelve tribes of Israel.
>
> "Simon, Simon, behold, Satan demanded to have you, that he might sift you like wheat, but I have prayed for you that your faith may not fail; and when you have turned again, strengthen your brethren." And [Peter] said to him, "Lord, I am ready to go with you to prison and to death." He said, "I tell you, Peter, the

cock will not crow this day, until you three times deny that you know me."

— Luke 22:28-34

I think that the present time offers a wonderful opportunity to the churches, all Christian denominations, and the other religions that believe that God is the Witness and Judge of all human beings, to speak out for the good of human nature. This is a God-given moment for all of us to ask ourselves whether we are making any real attempt to take a stand against the stupid paganism and hedonism that grips this country. The people who killed Jesus Christ were stupid people. They were stupid and wicked, and some of them were sadists. Similarly, the people who are destroying this country are stupid, some of them very stupid. In order to be very stupid, you have to be very smart. Ordinary stupidity is the prerogative only of those who have ordinary intelligence. Great stupidity presupposes great intelligence, enabling a person to do something greatly stupid. In the United States and other Western nations today there is, sad to say, great stupidity, and it is combined with great wealth and power — a potentially lethal mixture. What in the world is the matter with the United States? Why is it destroying its most precious natural resource — its youth? And what is the matter with the other countries of the world that they go along with this? Why do they consent by their silence to the pornography and gross public scandal that entice children and teenagers into immorality? What in the world is going on?

Again we quote from the Holy Father's address to Ambassador Nicholson:

> In order to survive and prosper, democracy and its accompanying economic and political structures must be directed by a vision whose core is the God-given dignity and inalienable rights of every human being, from the moment of conception until natural death. When some lives, including those of the unborn, are subjected to the personal choices of others, no other value or right will long be guaranteed, and society will inevitably be governed by special interests and convenience.
>
> Freedom cannot be sustained in a cultural climate that measures human dignity in strictly utilitarian terms. Never has it been more urgent to reinvigorate the moral vision and resolve essential to maintaining a just and free society.

Jesus says, "It must needs be that scandal come, but woe to that man by whom scandal shall come" (see Matthew 18:7). Abraham Lincoln cites those words in his second inaugural address, given during the depth of the Civil War. Alluding to the responsibility of the country for the injustice of slavery, he says, "Fondly do we hope, fervently do we pray, that this mighty scourge of war may speedily pass away. Yet if God wills that it continue until all the wealth piled by the bondsman's two hundred and fifty years of unrequited toil shall be sunk, and until every drop of blood drawn with the lash shall be paid by another drawn with the sword, as was said three thousand years ago, so still it must be said 'the judgments of the Lord are true and righteous altogether.' " I hope Lincoln was wrong in his estimate of divine justice, because the United States of America is legally responsible for the death of *fifty million* defenseless, innocent children.

What has to happen before we begin to face that responsibility? Unfortunately, a great many civil and political leaders are severely morally compromised by their support of abortion and its widespread practice. And, unfortunately, religious leaders have become compromised with them. When a prophetic voice here or there tries to say something about the evils of our time — pornography, abortion, euthanasia, the corruption of the young — we do not respond. Would we even listen to the prophetic voice of Jesus if He returned?

One of the friars of our community, Father Conrad Osterhout, who is our novice master, is a strong pro-life advocate. He was arrested in Lehigh County, Pennsylvania, in July 1991 and imprisoned from May 1992 to May 1993 in the county jail for protesting against abortion. Father Conrad and the other protesters were charged with trespassing and given sentences of from three to twelve months by a judge who said he was actually opposed to abortion personally, whatever that means. They would be released after three months if they would sign a paper and promise that they would not protest again. The treatment of Father Conrad during the time of his imprisonment is scandalous. On the feast of Corpus Christi, Father Conrad was asked to celebrate Mass with Father Harold Dagle, a priest who had been sent by the diocese of Allentown. Father Dagle asked Father Conrad to preside. Prison approval was received for both priests to offer Mass for the inmates. The officer in charge of the shift, who was called the shift commander, attended this Mass. He watched Father Conrad offer the Mass. After the other priests who had come for the Mass left, Father Conrad was taken to the prison office and charged with three criminal acts: holding an unauthorized gathering, receiving contraband (one of the priests had given him a rosary), and wearing a disguise (Mass vestments), which is considered an attempted escape. It is important to know that the guards were all there when he prepared for Mass and said Mass and that they had approved everything. Father Conrad and the others were subject to unusual restrictions during their confinement. Preparations were being made for them to work on a road gang repairing roads. They took this opportunity to protest the treatment they were receiving in the prison, which was excessively severe. As a result of this, they were put into administrative segregation and given the false reason that it was for their protection. Actually the prisoners were quite respectful to them. Father Conrad spent eleven months in this administrative segregation, which meant remaining in the cell for twenty-two hours a day. For fifteen days he was in disciplinary segregation, where he had no rights at all and could not receive phone calls or have visitors.

This was not Russia during Communist times. This was not China. This was Lehigh County, Pennsylvania, which is a reasonably civilized part of the country with a large Catholic population. The pathetic part is that there was no loud protest about this kind of treatment.

Shame, shame, shame on our country and its criminal justice system, which persecute protesters for life and completely failed to protect our national security. Recall, if you will, that about the time Father Conrad was in prison, the first attack on the World Trade Center occurred. If those who were in charge of our national security had pursued those attackers with the same vigilance and zeal they displayed when searching out those who protested the killing of children, it's quite possible that the World Trade Center might still be standing. These are painful facts to read, but they are facts.

There are relatively few voices raised in this country against immorality. The strongest voice against pornography in the media is that of a Baptist minister, Dr. Donald Wildmon, with his American Family Association down in Mississippi. He's really trying. He doesn't get much support, but he has mine.

Sadly, the United States will answer for the corruption of the young. Much of the world does not like the United States, because it sees us as a source of public immorality and cynicism about the value of family life. Most of us who live here try to live moral lives, but because of the media our public image as a nation is besmirched. Our community of friars and sisters work in New York City, which is in some ways a very unreligious and immoral place, but in other ways it is a very religious city. Thousands of people go to church in New York City every day. It can be a very prayerful city, with churches open at all hours for people to pray. Those from other parts of the country don't understand that about New York.

On the other hand, it is also true that New York controls much of the media — and the media are basically immoral, cynical, and sarcastic, and destructive of the young and of family life and values. According to figures released by the New York State Department of Health for 1999, about ten percent of all abortions in the United States were performed in the New York metropolitan area. This means about 120,000 deaths of unborn children. About half of these were performed in the city proper.

A number of articles have appeared recently in rather sophisticated publications in New York indicating that the quality of comedy has to change. They say that irony and cynicism are out. What has passed for irony was, in fact, the blackest cynicism. I can be ironic, but I'm not a cynic. And they are. They laugh at virtue. They mock the good. They even mock Mother Teresa and the Pope. They mock goodness in general. And they regret now that this cynicism has brought the wrath of much of the so-called third world down on them.

If you are a Christian, don't do what Peter did after the Last Supper. Do not deny Christ. Speak up. I appeal to the clergy of all monotheistic religions that universally believe that good must be done and evil must be avoided. If you are a member of the clergy and you believe in the Gospel, the Bible, or at least the natural law, *please* speak out, because this country has been on a very foolish picnic, a very dangerous immoral holiday.

Every day after the attacks, New Yorkers heard special radio advertisements inviting us to come to Broadway entertainment. We were told to put the recent tragedy behind us. We should go see a musical and feel better. The message is always the same: forget your troubles, distract yourself with some entertainment. What makes people think that the horrible destruction of life and property at the World Trade Center and the Pentagon and the crash of the plane in Pennsylvania were isolated incidents? Why should we assume that they were the first and only act of a ghastly drama? These were no isolated events. Already the specter of biological attack is all too obvious. When the attempt was made to blow up the World Trade Center eight years ago, the United States government did nothing. Nothing. We forgot our troubles and went back to seeing Broadway plays.

Look to history. There have been far worse disasters in the past than what happened in the

United States on September 11. We should remember the lessons of history. Rome was the most powerful of all empires. It wasn't the oldest, but it was the most powerful. The *pax Romana*, or peace of Rome, was enforced throughout much of Europe, western Asia, and northern Africa by war, death, terror, and crucifixion.

Jesus was crucified because the Jews were an enslaved people under the *pax Romana*, and crucifixion was the death reserved for slaves. Rome thought it was all-powerful and invincible. By the fourth century it got to be kind of half-baked Christian with many leftover pagans. And then Rome was sacked in 411 by Alaric, a barbarian king. Nobody could believe it. St. Augustine wrote *The City of God*, in which he warned Rome's pagans and half-baked Christians that for two hundred fifty years before the time of the Christian emancipation the Roman philosophers had been warning that the empire was in decline. Once Christians had a voice in public affairs after the end of the persecutions, they too warned the same thing over and over: Sts. Augustine, Jerome, John Chrysostom, and many others. Nobody listened, and Rome rotted to the core. We need to learn again the lessons of history.

According to Ferdinand Lot, the distinguished historian of the time, at no moment did the barbarian invaders exceed twenty percent of the population of the Roman Empire, but they took it over because it fell like a piece of decaying fruit into their hands. The Romans could not even defend themselves. The barbarians were unsophisticated and illiterate. They didn't even know how to send written messages, and they were racked by disease. They did not have advanced military equipment. Yet they took over the empire because they believed in life. The Romans believed in nothing but "Eat, drink, and be merry, for tomorrow we die." And so they did. America, learn the lessons of history.

I say to all the believing people in the United States, especially believing Christians, Jews, and Muslims, and most especially the clergy: Let's get down on our knees and ask ourselves, "What are we doing with all the blessings God has given us?" In his incisive study *Democracy in America*, written more than a century and a half ago, Alexis de

Tocqueville asked, "What will you do with all these things?"

We are wasting the blessings and gifts God has given us. We are wasting our most precious natural resource: our youth. The children whom we do not kill we corrupt.

Brothers and sisters, I know that these seem like harsh words and hard truths, but unless we learn something from this tragedy, it will be wasted suffering. Again I urge you to think of the face of the suffering Savior, who suffered for the world and paid for the sins of the world. He was innocent. The people in the World Trade Center and the Pentagon were not guilty people. They were hardworking people. They were all at their tasks, every last one of them, endeavoring to earn their daily bread and support their families.

I have visited a number of young families — widows and their children — filled with sorrow. Their fathers and mothers went to work on that September 11 and simply never came back. These families have scars that they will carry for the rest of their lives. Their suffering will be wasted unless America seriously repents and changes the immoral corruption of its own youth and the youth of the world.

In much the same way that the guilt of the world fell on the shoulders of Jesus Christ, so the guilt of the rich industrial nations fell on the people at the World Trade Center. They themselves were personally innocent. Let us pray fervently that they will be saved. Let us trust in the divine mercy that those who call on the name of the Lord in their last hour will be saved. "It shall come to pass that all who call upon the name of the LORD shall be saved" (Joel 2:32).

Remember to ask what you can do to help your church, your parish, your community, your country. Learn a valuable lesson or two from this dreadful attack on our country and our people. It did not come from the hands of God; it came from the hands of angry men. Some of the wrath was occasioned by the sins of our civilization. It has something to tell us about ourselves.

If we listen and pray, we can change.

Three

THE COUNTRY

"*If my people who are called by my name humble themselves, and pray and seek my face, and turn from their wicked ways, then I will hear from heaven, and will forgive their sin and heal their land.*"

— 2 Chronicles 7:14

*I*n the first chapter I spoke about the individual and the problem of evil, and the message of the life of Jesus Christ, our Divine Savior, who as Son of God endured the sufferings of life and of the world. Next we looked at the responsibility of Christianity, the Christian churches, and the clergy to use this act of terror as an opportunity to speak out against the gradual paganization of our society and particularly about the destruction of our youth. We see our country in severe moral decline. The recent attacks should be a wake-up call, especially for religion, so that it does not become the acolyte of evil. It's very important that we not go along with what is destructive to religious, Christian, and human values. We must not remain silent.

As we turn our attention to what these attacks mean for our country, I will be very critical of civil government in general and of the previous administration, which left us totally unprepared to defend ourselves and ward off the terrorists' attacks. The people who carried out this very well-planned attack were obviously unbalanced and motivated by a kind of paranoid homicidal religious fanaticism, if indeed their motivation can in any sense be called religious. But their actions were rather obvious even to casual observers. Unfortunately, our government was completely unprepared to deal at all with this highly suspicious behavior.

I have my own personal grievance against the federal and state governments, which ignored saboteurs and terrorists who had been operating for several years in the United States and who attempted to destroy the World Trade Center in 1993. Do you know who the government was watching? They were watching me and many others who are opposed to abortion. Some of us went to jail.

I was arrested, along with the very saintly Bishop George Lynch, eighty-three years old, and (at that time) Brother Fidelis Moscinski, who is now a priest in our Franciscan community. All we did was say the rosary. We didn't block anything. As we prayed at the entrance to the driveway of the abortion center, we stood on the public sidewalk. You could have driven a motorcycle between us. But we did deliberately stop walking during our prayer vigil. We knelt down to say the rosary on the sidewalk at the parking lot entrance.

Because Bishop Lynch and Brother Fidelis had been arrested more times than I had, they were brought up on federal charges by the federal attorney. I assume that the federal attorney brought the charges with some knowledge and connivance of the Attorney General, who at that time was Janet Reno. Judge John E. Sprizzo of the Federal District Court in Manhattan found Brother Fidelis and Bishop Lynch not guilty of violating a restraining order that he had issued, because they did not do so maliciously. The law requires that a violation must involve malicious intent. Judge Sprizzo cited the case of a Vietnam War protestor who was found not guilty because he had not made his protest maliciously.

Allow me to quote directly from the lead editorial in *The New York Times* of January 22, 1997, the day after the trial of Bishop Lynch and Brother Fidelis: "But instead of imposing sanctions for willfully violating his own order, Judge Sprizzo exonerated the men because they had acted out of religious conviction." That is not true. He said they acted without malice. I was in court and heard him. The *Times* editorial continued: "The judge's ruling is larded with dubious references to the Dred Scott decision, Nazi laws, and Bosnia, yet he fails to acknowledge that abortion is a protected right while the actions of the two defendants violate Federal law."

Do you know that abortion is the most protected right in the United States? I deny absolutely that there is equal justice before the law. A physician cannot give an aspirin to a minor without parental consent, but he can perform an abortion on a minor without consent of the parents. In the Abner Louima case, one hundred twenty-five people, many of them public officials, protested in front of the New York City Hall, blocking the entrance. Their actions were similar to ours except that they effectively blocked the entrance. We did not block any entrance. None of the City Hall demonstrators even got a ticket. In a local court, however, we were charged with disturbing the peace, which was not really even a misdemeanor; but Bishop Lynch at the age of eighty-three got fifteen days in jail and Brother Fidelis got ten. I got five, with time off for good behavior. It was obvious to anyone in the Dobbs Ferry, New York, court that day that the judge was taking her orders on sentencing us from the assistant district attorney.

Somebody asked me how we were treated in the Westchester County Jail in Valhalla, New York. I would have to say that we were treated like garbage. In a twenty-four-hour period we were strip-searched three times. On one of the very few occasions when any of the correctional staff spoke to us with any courtesy, two guards who had just strip-searched us said they had gone to a Catholic high school. They made a mistake in telling me this. I said to them, "You did this to a bishop of the Catholic Church? You are Catholics, and you admit that a bishop is a successor of the apostles. This man is eighty-three years old." Every correctional officer knows that exceptions are often made in prison. So much for equal protection before the law.

Certainly I abhor acts of terrorism anyplace. When our little group is in front of an abortion clinic, which we frequently are, we pray. We sing hymns. In a proper voice one of our group will offer a potential victim of abortion an opportunity for substantial help. As chairman of the board of the Good Counsel Homes, I am financially responsible for sixty-five homeless mothers and their babies. We are serious in our commitment to life and the protection of the lives of the unborn. We do not do unseemly things. Sometimes we say fifteen decades of the rosary. However, we did not receive equal protection under the law. At times — particularly some years ago in Dobbs Ferry — we were called vicious names. We were cursed at in the presence of the police. Extremely obscene gestures were openly made in the presence of the police. I am happy to say that the present police chief in Dobbs Ferry does not permit this kind of outrage. Years ago, however, no charges were ever made against those who did disturb the peace with obscenity and immodest behavior.

I ask you, "Where is our country headed?" I am very tired of seeing public officials intimidated by things that are wrong and illegal. Depriving a human being of life is wrong. When I read what happened in Nazi Germany in the 1930s, I wonder what I would have done if I had been there. Would I have been afraid? Probably. I received only a five-day sentence in Valhalla. Those who faced the Nazis got life or death in a concentration camp.

Our country is in very bad shape. Its laws protect severe immorality — the violation of human life. People will argue about whether a very young child in the womb is a human being, but what about a viable child at nine months who is already in the birth canal? If anyone can say that a child in the process of being born can be killed, then we are operating on totally different values. I question whether we as a nation can stay together, having on our national conscience the legal deaths of millions of children.

Politicians in our country are often intimidated into the approval of evil. Everyone agrees that people have a right to protest. I have protested war. I have often protested the deprival of human rights for African American people. I knew

Martin Luther King, Jr. I was with the parents of the brave young men who were missing as civil rights workers and who were later killed. But I am deeply distressed when politicians smile and clap for demonstrations that are obscene and uncalled for. If people feel that their rights are being violated or overlooked because of their sexual orientation, they have a perfect right to protest. They should take a lesson from the civil rights movement, the pro-life movement, and the peace movement. We could show them how to have a dignified, even prayerful demonstration. Unfortunately, there are gay rights parades in New York and other cities at which obscene sexual acts are performed or simulated in public, on the steps of St. Patrick's Cathedral. I have seen police officers deeply frustrated but forbidden to do anything. Yet people were doing things in public, which in any other circumstances would have resulted in their arrest. In our country it is a disturbance of the peace to openly mock someone else's person, religion, or values. And yet in front of St. Patrick's Cathedral every year people mock the Catholic Church and religious life without legal sanction.

They mock the religious habit, or garb, which I and many others cherish and wear proudly. They behave in obscene and disgraceful ways, wearing authentic liturgical vestments or religious garb. Such mockers are not religious at all, but they dress in mock religious habits with miniskirts to protest their grievances. Any group holding a demonstration should at least refrain from doing things that will alienate them from the rest of society. While a demonstration may not win some of us over to their point of view, it could, if conducted decently, at least cause people to think that they have the right to be left alone. Obviously I don't have to agree with someone's point of view or moral judgments in order to acknowledge their right to hold them peacefully.

I am told that the purpose of a gay rights demonstration is to convince us that homosexual behavior is normal. A bit of normal inoffensive behavior might be in order at the demonstrations. Sad to relate, just a few blocks from the cathedral, most of the city's politicians applaud these same demonstrators as they pass by in their parade. And they have just openly violated the law by disturbing the peace in front of the cathedral.

What is so distressing in the current politics of American life is the intimidation of politicians. How easily most of them are cowed by the morally indefensible demands of pro-abortion groups, even to the approval of partial-birth abortion. How quickly so many politicians, nominally Christian, accept — even actively court — these groups whose views not only violate basic Christian beliefs but also promote an agenda of hedonism and a culture of death. How few will speak in defense of the right to life, which in addition to being a sacred trust in Judeo-Christian culture, is a fundamental guarantee of the Declaration of Independence.

What has all this got to do with the tragedy at the World Trade Center? A great deal. Do we wonder why in whole countries of Asia there are mobs raging against the United States? Unquestionably these mobs are manipulated. Unquestionable too is that some of what they believe is untrue. People come from those countries to the United States, and if they have proper papers (or sometimes without), they are able to make their way up the social and economic ladder. Some will start as taxi drivers and end up doing quite well as property owners. That's the American dream. I don't know why anybody should be opposed to that. My relatives got off the boat with the shirts on their backs, and they did well. It can still be done. Perhaps it's even easier now.

Why, then, do so many people hate the United States? Partly because we are a very rich country, and we're very rich particularly because we're very greedy. Many of the saboteurs and terrorists were able to get into this country and make their way because of greed. When the terrorists were studying how to fly an airplane, why didn't anybody question why they wanted to know how to fly a plane but not want to know how to land or take off? Nobody asked questions because the terrorists were paying a great deal of money in cash for their lessons. It was a matter of greed. This country rots with greed. As St. Paul observes so well, the love of money is the root of all evil. It also rots with the political pressure that money buys.

Those of us who went to jail because we protested abortion did not get equal justice before the law. Earlier I mentioned how one of my confreres, Father Conrad, ended up in a form of solitary confinement called disciplinary segregation in the Lehigh County Jail after he asked and got permission to offer Mass, because he put vestments on over his prison uniform in the presence of the guards.

Do we give equal protection to unborn children? In some states we no longer give equal protection to the physically and mentally ill. Are we going to move into the nightmare of euthanasia as they have done in Holland, where the devout say that many unwilling people are being deprived of life? It's later than you think. We ourselves have been busy depriving inconvenient children of life but have been neglecting even our own national security.

When Father Fidelis and Bishop Lynch were tried, the federal attorneys responded to Judge Sprizzo's finding of not guilty by attempting to have them tried again. Did you take civics in high school? Surely you are familiar with the term "double jeopardy" and its meaning? When I was a sophomore in high school, I knew that double jeopardy violated the law. A person could not be tried again after being found not guilty. We should be able to assume that federal attorneys, working under the direction of the Attorney General, would be sufficiently informed about law to know, as even the American Civil Liberties Union reminded them, that you cannot try a person a second time for a crime if he has previously been found not guilty.

Were the hatred and disdain of the former administration so great against those who are pro-life that they eclipsed their legal judgment? I can find no other reason for *The New York Times* to imply in its editorials that my two co-defendants should be considered on a continuum with terrorists. The paper does not say that they are terrorists, but it puts them on a continuum with terrorists. It puts me there too by implication. And an article in the same *New York Times* a few years earlier called me a "saint," quoting a woman to whom I had given a Thanksgiving turkey. I am neither a saint nor a terrorist. Why does the FBI waste its resources by having a file on people like me? I know they do.

There is a strong bias in our country against speaking out for objective morality as there is for objective values. What could be more objective than the injustice of taking a human life? I was not only horrified but also heartbroken by the deaths of the people at the World Trade Center, and I know many families who suffered losses. No sane person takes any of this lightly. Like most New Yorkers, I have personally suffered with families and especially with children who were scarred for life by the terrorism. But we need to be reminded that in the United States every day thousands of children are deprived of life legally and with the connivance of many politicians.

The pro-life issue will not go away as the Supreme Court expected that it would in 1973. Those who are in favor of abortion, or at least of allowing abortion, will say that people have a right to make this choice. The basis of the Supreme Court decision in *Roe* v. *Wade* was that no one was able to make an ironclad case about abortion, because there was no agreement about when human life begins. God forbid that our courts should continue to operate with such logic, throwing objective morality to the wind in every case, because then the law would be nothing more than the opinion of lawyers. In fact, it was once thus described by Oliver Wendell Holmes, a profoundly antireligious and anti-Catholic judge whose legal philosophy continues to lead this country toward moral chaos.

Don't be afraid of criticizing the Supreme Court or any other court. Lawyers and journalists do it all the time. We can too. Don't be overly impressed by judges, even in very high courts. A judge is usually simply a lawyer who has a friend who is a politician.

We received a warning on September 11, and as citizens of this country we better pay attention to it. Each person should ask, "Am I part of the decline and fall of the second Roman Empire?" If you are, you will live in very unhappy times. The Western nations used to consider the United States their leader, but it has lost that place. For eight years our country wasted its prestige and failed to provide either political or moral leadership. In addition, it has failed completely to use the opportunities it had as the most powerful nation. What the United States has provided are economic and political arm twisting and intimidation. The President of Argentina, Carlos Menem, said that he had been threatened by the U.S. State Department during the previous administration with economic reprisals if he did not appoint representatives of pro-abortion groups to the women's conferences of the United Nations. Several delegates from African and Asian countries told our friars during a recent women's conference at the United Nations that they were receiving three hundred dollars a day expense money from pro-abortion groups in the United States. Again their governments have been strong-armed into appointing people who would vote for abortion. These delegates were ashamed to receive this aid because they knew that they had to support the pro-abortion and anti-family agenda at the United Nations.

I have hardly even alluded in this presentation to the other ugly smear on America's image before the world. We are the principal producers of pornography for youth around the world. Our media sets the moral tone for youth, and the tone is satanic. I have already discussed this earlier, but it needs to be restated here to complete the picture.

Our country exports pornography; it encourages euthanasia and abortion. Do you wonder why people hate us? And do you wonder that even nature itself begins to cry out? The people who died in the World Trade Center were innocent. They paid a price for a whole nation, perhaps for a whole civilization. Other innocent people may very well die, though God forbid. The specter of bioterrorism grips our country now, and it will not go away.

If you have to die, for heaven's sake die for what is good and holy. Die for what is a blessing to the world. Die for the honor and glory of God. Would you want to die in defense of what kills people and corrupts the young? Our nation has been given a call to repentance and conversion. Will the whole country or the whole civilization listen to it? Perhaps not. But I do believe in Jesus' words: "Every one who acknowledges me before men, I also will acknowledge before my Father who is in heaven" (Matthew 10:32).

I realize there are people in favor of abortion out of some distorted goodwill. Many of them think they're doing good and protecting human rights. I have often said to the pro-abortion demonstrators we meet in front of the clinics that we all have one thing in common — we think this is an important issue. I urge you to examine your conscience and ask yourself, "Is this a country that protects human life and protects the young?"

I often heard Mother Teresa say something I thought was puzzling: "The greatest obstacle to world peace is abortion." At first I did not see the connection. Then I realized that Muslims are generally very opposed to abortion, which they see as a violation of the commandment "Thou shalt not kill." The Muslim nations consistently vote against making legal abortion a requirement for membership in the United Nations. It was only as I watched in horror the imploding of the World Trade Center that I realized what Mother Teresa, a prophetess of our time, had really meant.

In 1975, in the last lecture he gave, the distinguished lay theologian Dietrich von Hildebrand, who had to leave Germany secretly shortly after the rise of the Nazis (he always referred to Hitler as "the criminal"), warned his audience, "A country that legalizes the murder of the innocent is doomed." He said these words with a voice trembling with emotion. We may now have the last opportunity to reverse this sentence.

I love my country with all its ills. I am delighted to see the signs around that say "God Bless America." We said it often in the past. Now I think we need to say "God help America" so that she can rise from the moral quicksand into which she has fallen.

Four

THE WORLD

"If I have told you earthly things and you do not
believe, how can you believe if I tell you heavenly
things? No one has ascended into heaven but he who
descended from heaven, the Son of man. And as
Moses lifted up the serpent in the wilderness, so must
the Son of man be lifted up, that whoever believes in
him may have eternal life."

For God so loved the world that he gave his only
Son, that whoever believes in him should not perish
but have eternal life.

— John 3:12-16

$\mathcal{W}$e have broadened our consideration of responses to the attacks of September 11 from the individual to the Church and the country. Now we take up the more complex question of the response of the world. When an attack on one's country occurs, like the recent acts of terror, many people suddenly feel the swelling of an emotional response, a powerful conviction, which some of them may not even recognize. It's called patriotism.

In the United States you would have to be at least fifty-five or sixty years old even to remember patriotism. I remember it as a boy during the Second World War. I recall many young men and women feeling honored to risk their lives in the battle against Nazism and fascism. Many of them died for their country. I recall the great surge of excitement when I stood near St. Paul's Chapel, close to the place where the World Trade Center was later built, and watched President Eisenhower

— then a general — coming down Broadway in a blizzard of ticker tape, waving his arms in the victory parade. The whole free world rejoiced.

But there's been a great deal of cynicism in the United States in recent decades, and we have fought wars that were not our own. Patriotism all but disappeared. Perhaps they were just wars or at least had just aspects to them. Who knows? But certainly young men and women did endanger and, in many cases, did sacrifice their lives to preserve their country. And they certainly hoped and believed that they were struggling for peace and a better world. Yet the cynicism that grips American life (and which may be about to disappear) kept them from even getting the respect that they had earned by risking their lives.

But suddenly patriotism is back. Flags are everywhere. Signs and posters proclaim, "God Bless America." We ask God's blessing on our country, but we cannot mention His name in a public school. His name is used in practically every political address by whoever makes it. God is constantly mentioned in public life but is banished from education. It's a form of schizophrenia, really. The country has a case of religious schizo-phrenia.

Other values surface when a whole society is in danger. I saw these values operate down at Ground Zero the night I worked in the morgue. There was an openness on the part of people to help one another. There's a camaraderie in the face of unspeakable disaster. There's sympathy and empathy for those who are bereaved. I can't tell you the sorrow that each of us felt when those who were going through the ruins would bring in a plastic bag containing human remains. How heartbreaking it all was for everyone involved. What does this say about the world we live in?

As we consider the significance that the at-tack should have for the world community, we think of course of the United Nations, with its headquarters only a couple of miles from the World Trade Center. My father was chief engineer for the Turner Construction Company when they erected the U.N. building. He used to ask, "What are we building?" The chairman of the General Assembly at that time was Dr. Belaunde of Ven-ezuela, a devout lay Franciscan. I asked him what the U.N. really was. He said to me, "It's a place for us to talk so that we do not fight."

Although the United Nations has only the authority that its members give it, which is scant enough, it began with an ideal of world peace. I am now deeply disturbed that the U.N. is constantly used by the wealthy nations as a vehicle for propagating violent behavior, especially abortion. Nonetheless, I still show visitors around the United Nations. There's the Meditation Room, with a remarkably beautiful stained-glass window by Marc Chagall. In that window are scenes from the whole Bible, Christian and Jewish — the birth, crucifixion, and death of Jesus, along with Moses and the Ten Commandments. Prominent in the window is a figure of St. Francis. And there are a number of religious symbols in the building: an Armenian cross, a mosaic dove from the old basilica of St. Peter, built around a thousand years ago, and a Buddhist bell. There's a remarkable statue on the grounds called the Triumph of Good over Evil, showing St. George killing a dragon made of ballistic missiles. This imposing work was given to the United Nations by the Soviet Union in the last year of the presidency of Mikhail Gorbachev to commemorate the nuclear nonproliferation treaty. It's the largest exterior religious statue in the city of New York.

The stated goal of the United Nations was indeed to bring peace to the world. It was for some an honest and sincere goal. The sincerity of individual member nations is hard to assess. The United Nations Charter called for mutual respect among nations and human rights. Obviously some members were very hypocritical because we know from information provided by the present Russian government that the rulers of Russia at that time were involved in mass murder. The Nazis, who had been involved in mass murder, had competitors, and some of them signed the United Nations Charter. But nonetheless, with a certain idealism, the U.N. went on.

I'd like to go back to that idealism. We need to respect one another. An extremely interesting article on Islam and the opposition of some Islamic leaders to terrorism by a professor of history at Harvard, Roy Mottahedeh, appeared in *The New York Times*. The professor points out that the people who perpetrated the acts of terrorism against the United States were uninformed about the real meaning of the Koran and Islamic law. He says:

> While some politicians and imperfectly educated Muslim clerics have used the word jihad — meaning holy war — in the sense of an armed struggle, in the same careless way some American leaders have used the word crusade. This meaning is rejected by most modern Muslim scholars who say that it properly refers to the struggle against the distortion of Islam that impedes the call to Islam.

From this article I understand that the jihad is actually a struggle within Islam, not a violent conflict with other religious groups. That's consoling to know. Certainly immense numbers of Islamic people in the world are horrified and embarrassed by these terrorists, as I would be if the terrorists in Northern Ireland represented me. They do not.

But we must all ask: "Do we teach children to

kill? Do we teach children hatred?" Morning, noon, and night, American television puts on programs for children that are about murder, war, and death.

When I was a youngster during World War II, I went to war movies like *Mrs. Miniver*, which was a great film. Those films were well done as part of the war effort. I cannot say I ever remember one that glorified war. Perhaps they glorified victory, but they were not sunk in death. And I went to see the antiwar films and the antitotalitarian films. I think perhaps the one that moved me the most was *The Pawnbroker*. I've never quite recovered from that film. Are we teaching children today about peace? About respect? About human love? About the family? About children?

I imagine that not many people have read St. Augustine's teaching on the just war. It's in Book 19 of *The City of God*. Augustine's teaching is most restrictive. It was not a formal teaching but rather a comment he made along the way, since nobody up to that time had ever asked whether any war was just.

For it is the wrongdoing of the opposing party which compels the wise man to wage just wars; and this wrongdoing, even though it gave rise to no war, would still be matter of grief to man because it is man's wrongdoing. Let everyone, then, who thinks with pain on all these great evils, so horrible, so ruthless, acknowledge that this is misery.

I know hardly any pacifist who couldn't go along with St. Augustine's definition of a just war. The just war would be one in which you have to protect your life or the life of someone else who is being attacked unjustly. On the other hand, what is abortion? It is the taking of an innocent life — a defenseless life — unjustly. When it comes to abortion, the discussion is filled with lies. What the world needs is a dose of truth. Christ says, "Seek the truth and the truth will make you free" (see John 8:32).

We are not free. We are compulsive, consumerist societies driven by a need for more of everything. It seems to go from the richest countries to the poorest countries. It is the challenge of religion — and most religions would admit this — to teach people that earthly possessions do not bring happiness. At best, they bring comfort. The best way for us to live on this little planet is to have a regard, and even a concern, for others, as well as for their needs and the needs of all on earth.

Recent political writers have been critical of the United States because, with its vast military power and wealth, it did not intervene effectively in the genocidal conflict that took place in Rwanda, a country obviously still struggling toward civilization. Did we Americans feel a responsibility for others there?

In our own country there are many people whose needs are not adequately cared for. I'm not talking about giveaways. One of the best things we've ever done for the poor — and I've worked for the poor all my life — is to provide them with a way to earn enough money to buy a little home of their own. I've seen the affordable-housing program bring peace to vast sections of New York City that once looked as if they had been bombed. A little bit of help for someone really trying to earn a living can have lasting effects. We need to be concerned for the world around us. St. Augustine is very clear in *The City of God* that as Christians we cannot avoid that responsibility. He sees it as flowing from the Sermon on the Mount and the parable of the Kingdom of God in the twenty-fifth chapter of the Gospel of St. Matthew: "I was hungry and you gave me food, . . . I was a stranger and you welcomed me" (verse 35). He tells Christians that we must work with all people of good-will to build a better society.

One of the things that Christians — especially those who love Sacred Scripture — are often preoccupied with are the prophecies of the endtimes. All sorts of people are telling me that the bombing of the World Trade Center is the beginning of the endtimes. I lived through World War II, and there were a couple of people around then who were very realistic candidates for the position of Antichrist. They were much more convincing as candidates than any of the people around right now. Osama bin Laden is responsible for the death of thousands. People like Joseph Stalin, who signed the United Nations Charter, were responsible for the death of tens of millions.

In spite of whatever has gone on in the past, we have a responsibility for God's daily judgment on the world we live in now. God's judgment is not like the judgment of men. It's not a decision. It's not an angry feeling. That's an anthropomorphism. God is infinite, absolute serenity — utter peace. St. Augustine says to God, "Ever laboring, you are ever at rest because you are your own peace."

When we go against God's goodness, tranquillity, truth, or peace, we become deeply disturbed and disoriented. Christians know that our only way out of that disturbance is the peace of Christ. But there are others who do not have faith in Christ who come to some peace as well. I would rather see a person look for God on another path but look earnestly with the only grace they have received than see a bad Christian who is not really seeking God at all. Christians are very quick at times to be critical of people of other religions but not of themselves. I heard that somebody once asked Gandhi, "What do you think of Christian civilization?" He answered, "It's a wonderful idea. They should try it."

If you're reading this, you may be Catholic, Protestant, Orthodox, or Jewish. You may be Muslim, Hindu, or Buddhist. As children of God, let us work for the triumph of good over evil, for a real observance of the law of nations. On the grounds of the United Nations is a bust of a man dressed in a religious habit much like my own. His name is Francisco de Victoria, and he was a Dominican friar who first wrote the Law of the Nations in the 1500s. The statue was placed there by the Spanish government. He wrote this law to promote world peace and also as part of the effort to get the Spanish explorers to observe and preserve the rights of the indigenous people they met in the New World. There was an ongoing conflict between the friars and the conquistadors about those human rights.

As Christians, and especially as Catholics, we know that seeking human rights is very much our responsibility because of the Gospel teaching. God's judgment does not only take place on that dramatic day at the end of the world. There will certainly be such a day, and Jesus speaks about it. There have been many judgment days in the past.

There have been judgments against Jerusalem, the Roman Empire, the Nazis, and the Communists. God's judgment doesn't save itself up for one big thundercloud. When the Nazis and the Bolsheviks came to their day of judgment, it was the result of their violating the natural law, the law of goodness, to such a degree that they destroyed themselves. They caused their own destruction, and their failure cannot be chalked up to anybody else's ingenuity. Their foolishness and greed brought them to destruction. Those who do evil today will come eventually to the same destruction. History is not filled with dramatic supernatural events with the sky opening and angels coming down to drag the Nazis off to hell. That's not what happened. They got to hell, but they got there on their own.

The judgment of God takes place every day, and it takes place in the human heart. Remember what Jesus says: "I did not come to judge the world but to save the world" (John 12:47). And He goes on to say that if some are judged, they have judged themselves. They have brought the judgment on themselves.

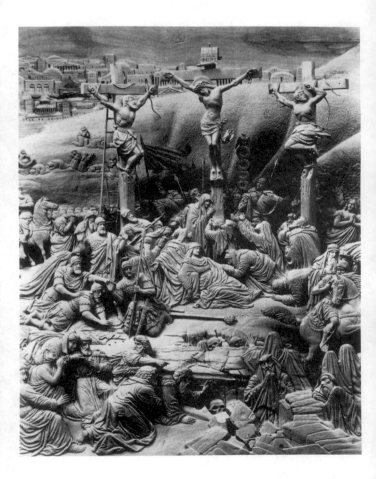

The cross of Jesus and the love of Jesus are at the center of human history for every Christian. Since the attacks of September 11, people have asked me, "How did God let it happen?" I recall again the words of Paul Claudel: "Jesus Christ did not come to take away all suffering, and He did not come to explain away all suffering. He came to fill all suffering by His presence." If you are a Christian, you should know He suffers with everyone.

There is a parable by Andrew Armstrong recounted in my little book *Arise from Darkness*. I have tried to find out who Andrew Armstrong is but without success. I feel sure that anyone who could write such a beautiful parable would not mind its being quoted.

All the people who had ever lived were assembled before the throne of God. They were a sullen lot. They all had complaints, and they began to murmur among themselves. Who does God think He is, anyway?

One of the groups was composed of Jews who had suffered persecution. Some had died in gas chambers and concentration camps — and they grumbled; how could God know of the suffering they had been through? Another group was slaves — black men and women with brands on their brows, great hosts of them, who had suffered indignities at the hands of those who called themselves "God's people" — What could God know about their plight? There were long lines of refugees driven from their lands — homeless people, who had nowhere to lay their heads. And there were poor people, who had never on this earth been able to make ends meet.

From each group a leader was chosen to draw up a case against the Almighty Himself. Instead of God judging them, they began judging Him. And the verdict was that God should be sentenced to live on earth as a human being with no safeguards to protect His divinity. And here was a bill of particulars:

Let Him be born a Jew. Let Him be born poor. Let even the legitimacy of His birth be suspect. Give Him hard work to do and poverty that He might know the pinch. Let Him be rejected by His people. Give Him for friends only those who are held in contempt. Let Him be betrayed by one of His friends. Let Him be indicted on false charges, tried before a prejudiced jury, convicted by a cowardly judge. Let Him be tortured, and then let Him die at the hands of His enemies.

As each group announced its sentence on God, roars of approval went up from the throng. Then everyone turned toward the throne. And suddenly heaven was filled with shocked penitent silence. For where there had been a throne, now could be seen a Cross.

Christians present our belief about Christ to the world in many different ways. They focus on Him as the Incarnate Word, the Savior and Redeemer, the Prince of Peace, the great King of the world to come. All these ways are valid enough. For me Jesus Christ is the God who suffers. He is the God who is here with us in our sufferings. We must see Him in the sufferings of others, of all the world. We must come to His aid as He suffers in all who are broken by sorrow.

That is why His cross must be seen at the

World Trade Center. Even if the mysterious steel cross had never been found there, the invisible cross bringing His suffering presence was there. In suffering humanity Jesus remains on the cross until the end of the world. This is the answer of Christ. It should be the answer that Christians give to all the world.

EPILOGUE

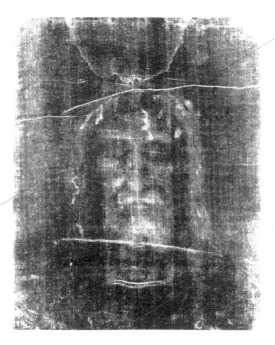

He fell to the ground and heard a voice saying to him, "Saul, Saul, why do you persecute me?" And he said, "Who are you, Lord?" And he said, "I am Jesus, whom you are persecuting."

— Acts 9:4-5

A Prayer to Christ Suffering With Us

*L*ord Jesus Christ, we know that as Son of God, You left the unchanging light of eternity to come into our dark world. By Your coming as a helpless child, You brought the light of hope to the struggling human race. By Your holy life and Gospel You taught us the way to live and die so as to live again forever.

Though You were totally innocent, by Your death You saved us through Your loving acceptance of the Father's will that You be as vulnerable as we are to the effects of evil and the darkness of sin. No one can now claim that God does not know what it means to suffer pain and injustice. You tasted it all, right down to the bitter dregs. You saw Your Mother and Your friends overwhelmed with sorrow, grief, and confusion. You even asked, "Why?"

And then when You departed and returned to the heavens, You mysteriously remained with us till the end of the world. Not only are You present in the sacraments and the Scriptures but You tell us that You are there with the sick, the poor, the suffering, and even the imprisoned. You weep with those who weep, You grieve with those who grieve, You die again with those who die or are killed. And Your cross, a cross made holy by suffering love, is the sign of all these mysteries, of all that love. While our lips cannot speak or our minds fathom all this mysterious truth, one word — the cross — sums it all up.

Have mercy on all who suffer, and especially those who suffered in the present darkness and attack. We hope, O Jesus, that all who died were called by You to Your Divine Mercy at the moment of death. Deliver our whole world from war and civil strife. Give us the truth and a love for justice. Send Your Holy Spirit that we may speak up for life and truth. And at the end of our days bring us to Your Father's house.

Lord Jesus Christ, place the sign of the cross on our troubled and suffering country, on the wounded human race stumbling along in blindness. Place the sign of the cross in the hearts of every one of us and let the light shining from the cross guide us on our way. Let all who come to You even in conflict and doubt, even in pain and bitterness, let them all know that Your cross is ultimately our only hope, the only sign of hope we need to guide us to eternal life, where we shall be together with You and the Father and the Holy Spirit. Amen.

Appendixes

Appendix One

POPE JOHN PAUL II

Following is the text of an address by Pope John Paul II at his general audience on Wednesday, September 12, 2001. He dispensed with his weekly catechetical instruction and devoted his talk to the subject of the terrorist attacks the day before in the United States.

A PAPAL ADDRESS CONCERNING THE ATTACKS IN THE UNITED STATES

I cannot begin this audience without expressing my profound sorrow at the terrorist attacks which yesterday brought death and destruction to America, causing thousands of victims and injuring countless people. To the President of the United States and to all American citizens I express my heartfelt sorrow. In the face of such unspeakable horror we cannot but be deeply disturbed. I add my voice to all the voices raised in these hours to express indignant condemnation, and I strongly reiterate that the ways of violence will never lead to genuine solutions to humanity's problems.

Yesterday was a dark day in the history of humanity, a terrible affront to human dignity. After receiving the news, I followed with intense concern the developing situation, with heartfelt prayers to the Lord. How is it possible to commit acts of such savage cruelty? The human heart has depths from which schemes of unheard-of ferocity sometimes emerge, capable of destroying in a moment the normal daily life of a people. But faith comes to our aid at these times when words seem to fail. Christ's word is the only one that can give a response to the questions which trouble our spirit. Even if the forces of darkness appear to prevail, those who believe in God know that evil and death do not have the final say. Christian hope is based on this truth; at this time our prayerful trust draws strength from it.

With deeply felt sympathy I address myself to the beloved people of the United States in this moment of distress and consternation, when the courage of so many men and women of good will is being sorely tested. In a special way I reach out to the families of the dead and the injured, and assure them of my spiritual closeness. I entrust to the mercy of the Most High the helpless victims of this tragedy, for whom I offered Mass this morning, invoking upon them eternal rest. May God give courage to the survivors; may he sustain the rescue workers and the many volunteers who are presently making an enormous effort to cope with such an immense emergency. I ask you, dear brothers and sisters, to join me in prayer for them.

Let us beg the Lord that the spiral of hatred and violence will not prevail. May the Blessed Virgin, Mother of Mercy, fill the hearts of all with wise thoughts and peaceful intentions.

Today, my heartfelt sympathy is with the American people, subjected yesterday to inhuman terrorist attacks which have taken the lives of thousands of innocent human beings and caused unspeakable sorrow in the hearts of all men and women of good will. Yesterday was indeed a dark day in our history, an appalling offense against peace, a terrible assault against human dignity.

I invite you all to join me in commending the victims of this shocking tragedy to Almighty God's eternal love. Let us implore his comfort upon the injured, the families involved, all who are doing their utmost to rescue survivors and help those affected.

I ask God to grant the American people the strength and courage they need at this time of sorrow and trial.

Pope John Paul II received the credentials of James Nicholson on September 13, 2001, as the new United States ambassador to the Holy See and gave the following address.

AMERICA'S MORAL POTENTIAL

Mr. Ambassador,

I am pleased to accept the letters of credence appointing you Ambassador Extraordinary and Plenipotentiary of the United States of America to the Holy See. You are beginning your mission at a moment of immense tragedy for your country.

At this time of national mourning for the victims of the terrorist attacks on Washington and New York, I wish to assure you personally of my profound participation in the grief of the American people and of my heartfelt prayers for the president and the civil authorities, for all involved in the rescue operations and in helping the survivors, and in a special way for the victims and their families.

I pray that this inhuman act will awaken in the hearts of all the world's peoples a firm resolve to reject the ways of violence, to combat everything that sows hatred and division within the human family, and to work for the dawn of a new era of international cooperation inspired by the highest ideals of solidarity, justice, and peace.

America's Heritage

In my recent meeting with President Bush I emphasized my deep esteem for the rich patrimony of human, religious, and moral values which have historically shaped the American character. I expressed the conviction that America's continued moral leadership in the world depends on her fidelity to her founding principles.

Underlying your nation's commitment to freedom, self-determination, and equal opportunity are universal truths inherited from its religious roots. From these spring respect for the sanctity of life and the dignity of each human person made in the image and likeness of the Creator; shared responsibility for the common good; concern for the education of young people and for the future of society; and the need for wise stewardship of the natural resources so freely bestowed by a bounteous God.

In facing the challenges of the future, America is called to cherish and live out the deepest values of her national heritage: solidarity and cooperation between peoples, respect for human rights, the justice that is the indispensable condition for authentic freedom and lasting peace.

Time of Great Possibilities

In the century now opening before us, humanity has the opportunity to make great strides against some of its traditional enemies: poverty, disease, violence. As I said at the United Nations in 1995, it is within our grasp to see that a century of tears, the twentieth century, is followed in the twenty-first century by a "springtime of the human spirit."

The possibilities before the human family are immense, although they are not always apparent in a world in which too many of our brothers and sisters are suffering from hunger, malnutrition, and the lack of access to medical care and to education, or are burdened by unjust government, armed conflict, forced displacement, and new forms of human bondage. In seizing the available opportunities, both vision and generosity are necessary, especially on the part of those who have been blessed with freedom, wealth, and an abundance of resources.

The urgent ethical issues raised by the division between those who benefit from the globalization of the world economy and those who are excluded from those benefits call for new and creative responses on the part of the whole international community. Here I would emphasize again what I said in my recent meeting with President Bush, that the revolution of freedom in the world must be completed by a "revolution of opportunity" which will enable all the members of the human family to enjoy a dignified existence and to share in the benefits of a truly global development.

Time of Great Dangers

In this context, I cannot but mention, among so many disturbing situations throughout the world, the tragic violence which continues to affect the Middle East and which seriously jeopardizes the peace process begun in Madrid. Thanks also to the commitment of the United States, that process had given rise to hope in the hearts of all those who look to the Holy Land as a unique place of encounter and prayer between peoples. I am certain that your country will not hesitate to promote a realistic dialogue which will enable the parties involved to achieve security, justice, and peace, in full respect for human rights and international law.

Mr. Ambassador, the vision and the moral

strength which America is being challenged to exercise at the beginning of a new century and in a rapidly changing world call for an acknowledgment of the spiritual roots of the crisis which the Western democracies are experiencing, a crisis characterized by the advance of a materialistic, utilitarian, and ultimately dehumanized worldview which is tragically detached from the moral foundations of Western civilization.

Culture of Life

In order to survive and prosper, democracy and its accompanying economic and political structures must be directed by a vision whose core is the God-given dignity and inalienable rights of every human being, from the moment of conception until natural death. When some lives, including those of the unborn, are subjected to the personal choices of others, no other value or right will long be guaranteed, and society will inevitably be governed by special interests and convenience.

Freedom cannot be sustained in a cultural climate that measures human dignity in strictly utilitarian terms. Never has it been more urgent to reinvigorate the moral vision and resolve essential to maintaining a just and free society.

America's True Wealth

In this context my thoughts turn to America's young people, the hope of the nation. In my pastoral visits to the United States, and above all in my visit to Denver in 1993 for the celebration of World Youth Day, I was able personally to witness the reserves of generosity and goodwill present in the youth of your country.

Young people are surely your nation's greatest treasure. That is why they urgently need an all-round education which will enable them to reject cynicism and selfishness and to grow into their full stature as informed, wise, and morally responsible members of the community.

At the beginning of a new millennium, young people must be given every opportunity to take up their role as "craftsmen of a new humanity, where brothers and sisters — members all of the same family — are able at last to live in peace" (Message for the 2001 World Day of Peace, 22).

Mr. Ambassador, as you begin your mission as your country's representative to the Holy See, I reiterate my hope that in facing the challenges of the present and future, the American people will draw upon the deep spiritual and moral resources which have inspired and guided the nation's growth, and which remain the surest pledge of its greatness.

I am confident that America's Catholic community, which has historically played a crucial role in the education of a responsible citizenry and in the relief of the poor, the sick, and the needy, will be actively present in the process of discerning the shape of your country's future course.

Upon you and your family and all the American people I cordially invoke God's blessings of joy and peace.

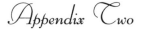

EDWARD CARDINAL EGAN, ARCHBISHOP OF NEW YORK

Following is the homily given by His Eminence at St. Patrick's Cathedral on September 17, 2001.

HOMILY AT THE MASS FOR THE DECEASED POLICE OFFICERS, FIRE FIGHTERS, HEALTHCARE AND EMERGENCY SERVICE WORKERS

My dear friends:

On the road to Assisi, the town of St. Francis, there is a little fifteenth-century chapel at which tourist buses occasionally stop. There is nothing of great artistic merit in this chapel. It is like many another in that province of Italy which is known as Umbria.

There is, however, just inside the door on the left, a crucifix which, even if it not be a great work of art, has an important message about death to deliver to all who see it.

It is almost life-size, heavily varnished, and very old; and it can be easily missed in the darkened interior of the chapel unless a guide points it out. In fact, most guides who lead visitors to the chapel have them assemble in front of the crucifix and shine a flashlight up into it so as to reveal its wonder.

The light is first directed to the left side of the face of the crucified Savior. The brow is deeply furrowed. The mouth is twisted. The Son of God Made Man is clearly in torment.

The guide then moves to the right side, shines the light again into the face of the Lord, and the impression one receives on this side is altogether different. The face is at peace. There is on it even a suggestion of triumph.

Visitors inevitably ask the guide to repeat the process. They marvel at what they see, and soon they become aware of the lesson the crucifix is teaching. Death, it proclaims, has, and must have, two faces — one of sadness and pain and the other of peace and triumph.

This evening, here in our beloved Cathedral, there is in our midst much sadness and pain. Families and friends have lost men and women whom they dearly loved and who dearly loved them. The loss was sudden and unexpected. Those taken from us were healthy and strong and often quite young. They were skilled and disciplined. They were full of life and full of hopes. They had wondrous plans for the future. They had mothers and fathers, husbands and wives, brothers and sisters, sons and daughters, comrades and friends, with all of whom they looked to share many happy, loving years.

They are no longer with us, and we are hurting.

But we dare not stand on only one side of the crucifix. We need to move to the other side and see the other face of the Savior as well.

Who are these men and women that we mourn? They are police officers, fire fighters and healthcare and emergency service workers who dedicated their lives to serving the community in which they lived. They guided us. They protected us. They gave their lives for us.

St. John the Apostle puts all of this in focus with just a few words from the First Reading of this Mass. Those who do not love, he tells us, are in a sense already dead; and those who love so intensely as to give their lives for others will live forever with their God.

Jesus Christ, our Lord and Savior, made this crystal clear on Calvary's cross. He was divine, but He took on our humanity to die for us simply because He loved us. This, St. John continues, is how we are to learn the true meaning of love — from the Son of God Who gave His life for others.

Such too, my dear friends, are those whom we mourn and celebrate in this Holy Mass. Criminals of the worst kind attacked innocent people. They killed thousands. They injured hundreds. They brought immense sorrow into the hearts and lives of millions. And who was there to face them down? Who was there to defend us? Who was there to shield us? Who was there to rescue all who could be rescued? We know full well. They are called police officers. They are called fire fighters. They are called healthcare and emergency service workers. And tonight we call them heroes.

We contemplate their passing, and we see much more than sadness and pain. We see peace. For they were men and women of peace who gave us peace. However, even more, in them we see triumph.

All of us have our fears. These heroes of ours had theirs too. But they conquered them. Millions of tons of stone and steel were falling all about them. Hurricanes of dirt, dust, and debris were engulfing them. There was no light with which to see. There was no air with which to breathe. All the same, they did what they always did. They guided, they protected, they defended, they shielded, and they rescued. And in so doing they handed over their lives for the safety and well-being of others. If this is not triumph, I do not know what triumph might be. Triumph over fear. Triumph over caring only for oneself. Triumph over all that makes us less than what the Lord would have us be. Triumph that defines heroes — wondrous, glorious heroes.

This evening I stand here in this pulpit as a citizen of a great City whose heart is heavy, indeed, whose heart is broken because we have lost so many of the best among us. I promise the mothers and fathers, husbands and wives, the brothers and sisters, the sons and daughters, the friends and comrades of our heroes that I will never forget what these gallant police officers, fire fighters, and healthcare and emergency service workers have done. As long as I live, they will have a very special place in my Masses and my prayers.

And the same will be true of the loved ones whom our heroes left behind. I will speak with the Lord about them regularly. I will ask Him to console them. I will ask Him to give them peace. I will ask Him to keep them ever in His Love.

Nor will I ever have any doubt that my prayers will be answered. For the words of the Lord in the Gospel of this Mass are marvelously clear. "Come to Me," He says to all who are weary, burdened, and hurting. "Come to Me. I will refresh you."

This evening we do precisely this. We come to Him. We gather around the altar and we receive Him — Body, Blood, Soul, and Divinity — into our own hearts and souls. We speak with Him. He speaks with us. He tells us that He loves us. He tells us that He loves those whom we mourn.

He comforts us. He strengthens us. He reminds us that He is "meek and humble of heart," and He promises to lighten our burden.

We decide to remain on the right side of the crucifix. We look up into the face of the Redeemer. We are at peace. We rejoice in His triumph over sin and death, and we rejoice in the triumph of our loved ones as well.

O my Savior, we pray, thank You for the heroes whom You gave us. Thank You for love and inspiration that they gave us. Your grace will always be sufficient for us. We are not afraid. We are strong. We are Yours, at peace, and sharing in the triumph of our heroes. Wrap them and us in Your arms and Your love forever. Amen.

Appendix Three

ST. FAUSTINA

The following is taken from Conversations with the Merciful God from the Diary of Blessed [now Saint] Maria Faustina, *published in 2000 by the Marian Press in Stockbridge, Massachusetts.*

CONVERSATION OF THE MERCIFUL GOD WITH A DESPAIRING SOUL

JESUS: **O soul steeped in darkness, do not despair. All is not yet lost. Come and confide in your God, who is love and mercy.**

But the soul, deaf even to this appeal, wraps itself in darkness.

Jesus calls out again:

My child, listen to the voice of your merciful Father.

In the soul arises this reply: "For me there is no mercy," and it falls into greater darkness, a despair which is a foretaste of hell and makes it unable to draw near to God. Jesus calls to the soul a third time, but the soul remains deaf and blind, hardened and despairing. Then the mercy of God begins to exert itself, and without any cooperation from the soul, God grants it final grace. If this too is spurned, God will leave the soul in this self-chosen disposition for eternity. This grace emerges from the merciful Heart of Jesus and gives the soul a special light by means of which the soul begins to understand God's effort, but conversion depends on its own will. The soul knows that this, for her, is final grace and, should it show even a flicker of good will, the mercy of God will accomplish the rest:

My omnipotent mercy is active here. Happy the soul that takes advantage of this grace.

JESUS: **What joy fills My Heart when you return to Me. Because you are weak, I take you in My arms and carry you to the home of My Father.**

SOUL (*as if awakening, asks fearfully*): Is it possible that there yet is mercy for me?

JESUS: **There is, my child. You have a special claim on My mercy. Let it act in your poor soul;**

let the rays of grace enter your soul; they bring with them light, warmth, and life.

SOUL: But fear fills me at the thought of my sins, and this terrible fear moves me to doubt Your goodness.

JESUS: **My child, all your sins have not wounded My Heart as painfully as your present lack of trust does — that after so many efforts of My love and mercy, you should still doubt My goodness.**

SOUL: O Lord, save me Yourself, for I perish. Be my Savior. O Lord, I am unable to say anything more; my pitiful heart is torn asunder, but You, O Lord . . .

Jesus does not let the soul finish but, raising it from the ground, from the depths of its misery, He leads it into the recesses of His Heart where all its sins disappear instantly consumed by the flames of love.

JESUS: **Here, soul, are all the treasures of My Heart. Take everything you need from it.**

SOUL: O Lord, I am inundated with Your grace. I sense that a new life has entered into me and, above all, I feel Your love in my heart. That is enough for me. O Lord, I will glorify the omnipotence of Your Mercy for all eternity. Encouraged by Your goodness, I will confide to You all the sorrows of my heart.

JESUS: **Tell me all, My child, hide nothing from Me, because My loving Heart, the Heart of your Best Friend, is listening to you.**

SOUL: O Lord, now I see all my ingratitude and Your goodness. You were pursuing me with Your grace, while I was frustrating Your benevolence. I see that I deserve the depths of hell for spurning Your graces.

JESUS *(interrupting)*: **Do not be absorbed in your misery — you are still too weak to speak of it — but rather gaze on My heart filled with goodness, and be imbued with My sentiments. Strive for meekness and humility; be merciful to others, as I am to you; and when you feel your strength failing, if you come to the fountain of mercy to fortify your soul, you will not grow weary on your journey.**

SOUL: Now I understand Your mercy, which protects me and, like a brilliant star, leads me into the home of my Father, protecting me from the horrors of hell that I have deserved, not once, but a thousand times. O Lord, eternity will hardly suffice for me to give due praise to Your unfathomable mercy and Your compassion for me.

Appendix Four

JOHN HENRY NEWMAN

The following, by John Henry Newman, is taken from Parochial and Plain Sermons, VI, Sermon 7, *and cited in* Arise from Darkness (*Ignatius Press, 1987*).

How to Understand Life

Ten thousand things come before us one after another in the course of life, and what do we think about them? What color do we give them? Are we to look at all things in a gay and mirthful way? or in a melancholy way? in a desponding or a hopeful way? Are we to make light of life altogether, or to treat the whole subject seriously? Are we to make greatest things of little consequence, or least things of great consequence? Are we to keep in mind what is past and gone, or are we to look to the future, or are we to be absorbed in the present? *How* are we to look at things? [In contemporary language we would say, "What is our attitude toward life?"] This is the question which all persons of observation ask themselves, and answer each in his own way. They wish to think by rule; by something within them, which may harmonise and adjust what is without them. Such is the need felt by reflective minds. Now, let me ask, what *is* the real key, what is the Christian interpretation of this world? What is given us by revelation to estimate and measure this world by? The event of this season, — the Crucifixion of the Son of God.

It is the death of the Eternal Word of God made flesh, which is our great lesson how to think and how to speak of this world. His Cross has put its due value upon every thing which we see, upon all fortunes, all advantages, all ranks, all dignities, all pleasures, upon the lust of the flesh, and the lust of the eyes, and the pride of life. It has set a price on the excitements, the rivalries, the hopes, the fears, the desires, the efforts, the triumphs of mortal man. It has given a meaning to the various, shifting course, the trials, the temptations, the sufferings of his earthly state. It has brought together and made consistent all that seemed discordant and aimless. It has taught us how to live, how to use this world, what to expect, what to desire, what to hope. It is the tone into which all the strains of this world's music are ultimately to be resolved. . . . The doctrine of the Cross of Christ does but anticipate for us our experience of the world. It is true, it bids us grieve for our sins in the midst of all that smiles and glitters around us; but if we will not heed it, we shall at length be forced to grieve for them from undergoing their fearful punishments. If we will not acknowledge that this world has been made miserable by sin, from the sight of Him on whom our sins were laid, we shall experience it to be miserable by the recoil of those sins upon ourselves.

About the Author

Internationally known lecturer and retreat master Father Benedict J. Groeschel, C.F.R., is professor of pastoral psychology at St. Joseph's Seminary in New York. The director of the Office for Spiritual Development of the Archdiocese of New York, he is also a founding member of the Franciscan Friars of the Renewal. A prolific author and regular guest on EWTN, Father Benedict is the founder of Trinity Retreat, a center of prayer and study for the clergy.